FAIR OAKS ELEMENTARY SCHOOL
407 BARBER ROAD
MARIETTA, GA. 30060

AFRICAN MYTHS

Neil Morris

Skyview Books

an imprint of

WINDMILL BOOKS
New York

Published in 2009 by Windmill Books, LLC
303 Park Avenue South, Suite # 1280, New York, NY 10010-3657

Series concept: Alex Woolf
Editor: Alex Woolf
Illustrators: Fiona Sansom and Graham Kennedy
Designer: Ian Winton

        Publisher Cataloging Data

Morris, Neil, 1946-
        African myths / Neil Morris ; [illustrators, Fiona Sansom and
Graham Kennedy].
                p.   cm. – (Myths from many lands)
        Includes bibliographical references and index.
        Summary: This book provides a brief introduction to early African civilization,
a retelling of fifteen African myths, and a who's who of characters.
ISBN 978-1-60754-215-5 (library binding)
ISBN 978-1-60754-216-2 (paperback)
ISBN 978-1-60754-217-9 (6-pack)
        Tales—Africa   2. Folklore—Africa   3. Mythology, African—Juvenile
literature   [1. Folklore—Africa   2. Mythology, African]   I. Sansom, Fiona
II. Kennedy, Graham   III. Title   IV. Series
        398.2/096—dc22

Printed in the United States

CONTENTS

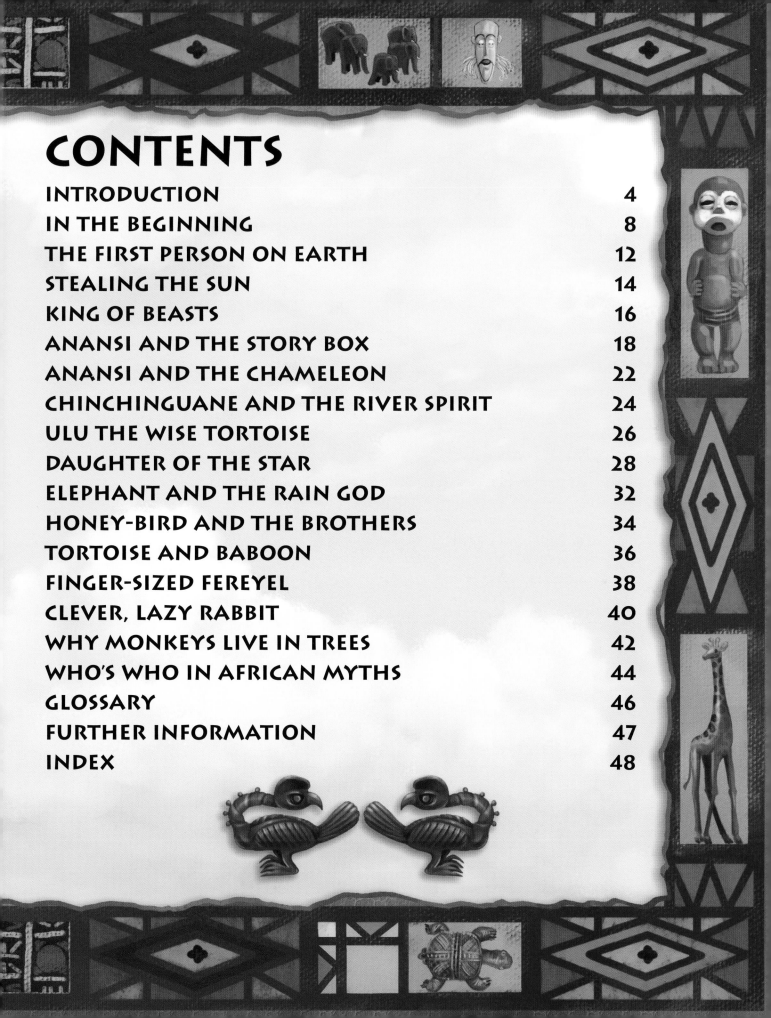

INTRODUCTION

The continent of Africa is often called the birthplace of human beings. We believe that the first humans were born there in prehistoric times. Early Africans lived as hunter-gatherers, moving around in search of food. There were animals to hunt and plants to gather.

THE FIRST FARMERS

Eventually, some people began planting seeds to grow crops such as corn, and they started staying in one place and became farmers. They also learned to herd animals and keep them in fields.

DIFFERENT CULTURES

Different groups of African people formed separate traditions and ways of life. They spoke different languages, and today more than 800 languages are

MEDITERRANEAN SEA

SAHARA DESERT

NIGER

NILE

LAKE CHAD

CONGO

AFRICA

LAKE VICTORIA

LAKE TANGANYIKA

LAKE MALAWI

ZAMBEZI

N
W E
S

spoken in Africa. About 300 of these belong to the Bantu family of languages. Many of those who speak a Bantu language are descendants of people who started to move from northwest Africa to the central forests about 2,000 years ago.

THE AFRICAN CONTINENT

The different peoples of Africa were influenced by their surroundings. Much of the continent is desert, including the world's largest, the Sahara Desert. Much of the rest of Africa is covered by rainforest, woodland or rolling grassland called savannah. People grouped together in villages and their way of life, especially their food, depended on their environment.

MYTHS AND STORIES

People's beliefs and myths varied from place to place, because they were based on personal experiences.

Hunting and herding groups told stories of animals, turning them into characters that act like humans. In some areas, the tortoise was considered the smartest animal. In other regions, it was the hare or rabbit. Myths about the creation of the world were similar across the continent, though the names of the creator gods varied in different languages.

African myths were passed on down the generations, as older people told the stories to youngsters. The myths were not written down. Some may have been forgotten, and others have changed over the years. The myths that exist still delight listeners and readers today.

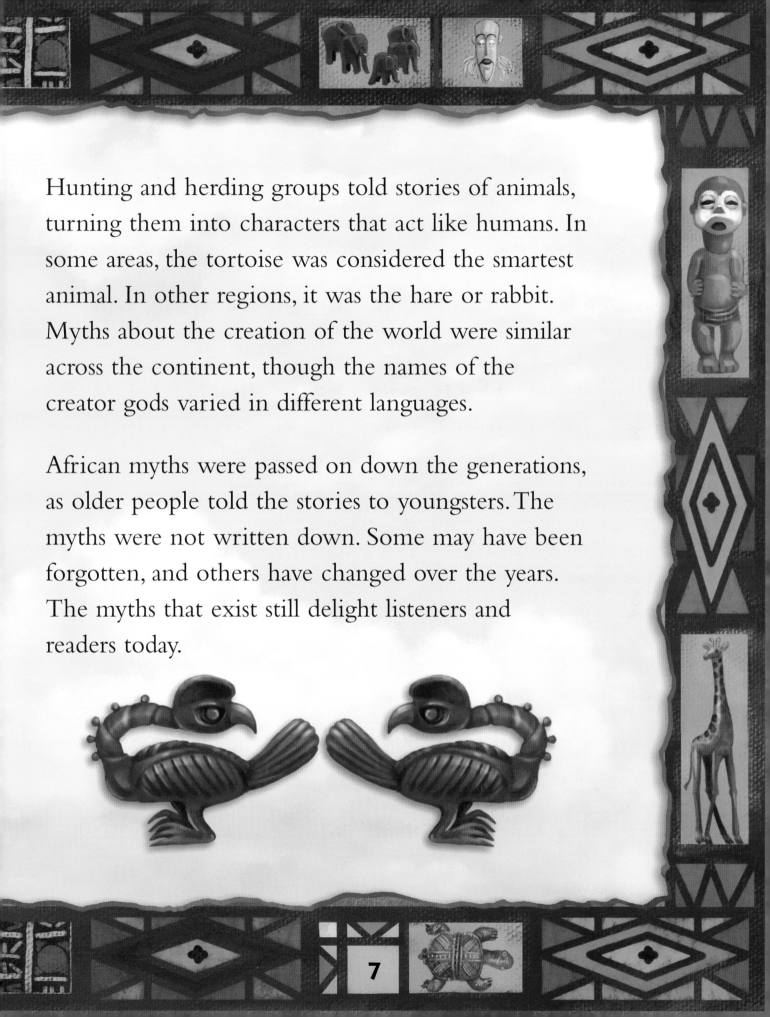

IN THE BEGINNING

At the very beginning of time, the sky god Olorun created the universe. He lived in the heavens with his wife and their son Obatala. Olorun also made other gods, and one of these was called Olokun. She ruled the vast ocean that lay beneath the sky.

As time passed, young Obatala grew tired of looking down on nothing but the ocean. He asked his father if he could make something new. The sky god gave his permission and advised his son to visit Orunmila, the god of wisdom. Orunmila told the young god to collect five things – a golden chain, a snail's shell filled with sand, a chicken, a palm nut, and a cat. Then he told Obatala what to do with these things.

First Obatala collected gold and took it to Ogun, the god of metalwork, who forged it into a long chain. Obatala let the chain down toward the waters below.

Then Obatala found a snail's shell, filled it with sand and turned it over so that the sand fell onto the water. This made islands, which quickly grew into large areas of land.

Next Obatala released the chicken, which fluttered down and started scratching at the land, making hills and valleys.

Obatala jumped down from the chain and planted the palm nut, which grew into one palm tree, then another and another. Obatala decided to live beside the palm trees, with the cat to keep him company. Then he dug in the sand for clay and molded some figures with it. When the figures were ready, Olorun breathed life into the first people on earth.

Everyone was happy, except for Olokun. The sea goddess did not like all this new land in her ocean and angrily whipped up huge waves. These flooded the land, until Orunmila put a stop to it. He cast a magic spell that made all the floodwater flow back to the ocean. Life on dry land could begin.

THE FIRST PERSON ON EARTH

The first person on earth was called Kintu. All the young man had was a cow, who gave him milk. One day the sky god's daughter, Nambi, saw Kintu and fell in love with him. When she asked her father's permission to marry, the god said Kintu must prove his worth.

Nambi's brothers stole Kintu's cow and took it up to heaven. Kintu had never eaten anything but milk, but he soon found roots and berries. Then Nambi took Kintu up to heaven, where her brothers gave him many tests. He passed them all. Finally their father asked Kintu to pick out his own cow from the huge heavenly herd. As the young man thought about this, a bee buzzed by and said he would help.

The bee soon settled on one of the cows' horns. "That is my cow," said Kintu. Nambi's father laughed and gave the couple his blessing. They returned to earth, where they planted crops and had many children.

13

STEALING THE SUN

Bokele's village was always dark. But the young man had heard of the light of the sun and was determined to find it. As he set off in his canoe, Mouse ran up and asked to help. Then Turtle appeared, followed by Hawk and, finally, a swarm of wasps. Bokele wondered how they could all help, but allowed them to go with him.

After a long river journey, Bokele reached a village deep in the rainforest. Mouse scampered off at once. He soon came back and said he had heard people whispering about a great light in a cave. Turtle trundled off and found the cave. Then Hawk flew in, grasped the sun and soared off to the canoe.

As Bokele paddled home with the sun, the cave's guards chased and attacked him. But the wasps came straight to the rescue, stinging the guards and fighting them off. And that is how the animals helped Bokele steal the sun.

KING OF BEASTS

Lion was eating too many of the other animals, so they asked him to eat just one of them each day. When the animals said they would make this easy for him, the lazy King of Beasts agreed.

The animals drew straws to see whose turn it was to be eaten. First was Antelope, followed by Warthog, then Guinea Fowl. Next it was Hare's turn.

On the chosen day, Lion searched everywhere for Hare. At last he found him, sitting in a tree overlooking a well. "Another lion wanted to eat me," Hare explained, "so I climbed up here. He says he's much stronger than you!"

"Where is this fool?" growled Lion.
"He's down in the well," Hare replied.

Lion looked down and saw another big cat reflected in the water. Furious, he sprang at his rival – and drowned in the well.

Hare sauntered off to tell the other animals that there was a new King of Beasts – himself!

ANANSI AND THE STORY BOX

One day, Anansi the spider went to the sky god and asked to buy his story box. "To pay for it, you must bring me a python, a leopard, a bush spirit and a swarm of hornets," the sky god said.

Anansi went home and asked his wife's advice. She gave him a long stick and twine, and sent him down to the river. On his way, Anansi saw a python curled up in the sun. He told the snake that his wife said no python was longer than his stick. "Measure me," said the python proudly, stretching himself right out. But instead of measuring, Anansi tied the snake to the stick so that he couldn't move.

Then Anansi's wife told him to dig a deep pit. That's how he trapped and killed a leopard. But how could he possibly catch a bush spirit? His wife told him how. Anansi had to carve a large wooden doll, cover it with sticky sap and place it near a tree where bush spirits lived.

Soon a spirit came and asked the doll what it was doing. When the spirit got no reply, it slapped the doll and its hand stuck. So it slapped with the other hand, and that stuck too. Soon the bush spirit could not move.

Anansi had no idea how to catch hornets. But his wife did. The spider went off in search of a hornets' nest, and when he found one, he splashed it with water. The hornets buzzed out angrily. "Come and shelter from the rain," said Anansi, holding out a gourd. When the hornets flew in, Anansi stopped it up with leaves.

Anansi took the python, leopard, bush spirit and hornets to the sky god. "Many others have tried and failed," said the god, "but you have paid the price. The story box is yours." Since that day, Anansi and his wife have known all the world's stories.

ANANSI AND THE CHAMELEON

Anansi the spider was a trickster and he thought he could outwit anyone. One year, when his harvest was not so good, Anansi decided to take over Chameleon's little field. The lizard complained to the other villagers, but no one would listen. So he plotted his revenge.

Chameleon dug a very deep pit, covered it with a roof and left just a tiny hole for a door. Then he caught hundreds of flies, tied them to dried vines and made a brilliant cloak that shone and buzzed in the sun. When Anansi saw the cloak, he had to have it. Chameleon said he would sell it for a store full of grain. Anansi agreed and ordered his sons to pour grain into Chameleon's tiny storeroom. But they poured and poured, for days and weeks, until Anansi had no food left.

All the villagers laughed at Anansi the spider, and ever since then he has hidden in the corners of houses.

CHINCHINGUANE AND THE RIVER SPIRIT

Chinchinguane was a chief's favorite daughter. The chief and all his villagers were sad when one day she drowned in the river. But Chinchinguane was not really dead. She had been swallowed by a giant fish, the river spirit. He turned her into a fish, and though she could see her sisters from the river, she could not speak to them.

The little fish was so sad without her family that the spirit took pity on her. He gave her a magic wand, and when she slid out of the water, her fish scales turned into a dress of silver coins. The girls were delighted to have their sister back.

The next day, all the sisters were out in the
forest collecting firewood when they came
across a group of one-legged ogres. As they ran
away, Chinchinguane touched
the ground with her wand
and a great river surged
behind them. Safe from the
ogres, Chinchinguane
knew
who had rescued them
– the river spirit.

ULU THE WISE TORTOISE

One day a hunter met a forest demon, who demanded half his catch. Seeing the demon's sharp claws and teeth, the hunter cut his catch in half and handed it over. From then on, the same thing happened every day.

The hunter's wife was unhappy at losing half her meat and insisted on going hunting with him. They soon met the demon, who demanded half the man's wife! The hunter refused, but the demon insisted she looked tasty to eat and he must have his share.

Luckily, Ulu the wise tortoise overheard the dispute and offered to help.

"Do you like your meat cooked?" the tortoise asked.

"Of course!" bellowed the demon.

"Then go to the river and fetch water for your cooking pot," said Ulu.

As the demon rushed off, Ulu told the hunter and his wife to run back to their village. They did, and were so grateful that they and their people never caught or ate tortoise again.

DAUGHTER OF THE STAR

There was once a king who loved watching stars in the night sky. One bright star was his favorite, and he thought to himself, "If only that beautiful star were a woman, then I could marry her!"

The next evening, after sunset, a beautiful young woman came to visit him. "My name is Nyachero, daughter of the star," she said. "Last night you said you wanted to marry me." The king was overjoyed.

He married Nyachero at once, and they lived happily together.

Some months later, Nyachero told her husband that she was going to have a baby and would like to visit her parents. The king agreed, appointing twelve of his best men to guard the queen on her way. Nyachero and the guards were carried up to the heavens on a cloud. When they reached the land of stars, she showed the men to her old house. There were chairs, beds and three large pots in the corner of the room.

Nyachero invited the men to rest after their journey, while she went to greet her parents. "Soon I will bring food," she said. "Meanwhile, whatever you do, do not open any of the pots."

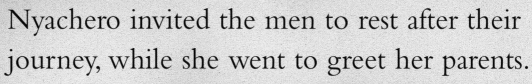

Soon the guards grew hungry. One of them decided to open a pot, to see if there was food inside. When he took off the lid, a cloud of mosquitoes flew out and stung them all.

The men at last beat them off, but soon grew hungry again.

When one of them opened the second pot, a cloud of locusts flew out and smothered them. The men beat them off, but soon grew hungry again.

When one of the men opened the third pot, a cloud of flies flew out and swarmed around them. The men at last beat them off, and were glad when it was time to return home. But ever since that day, flying insects have plagued people down on earth.

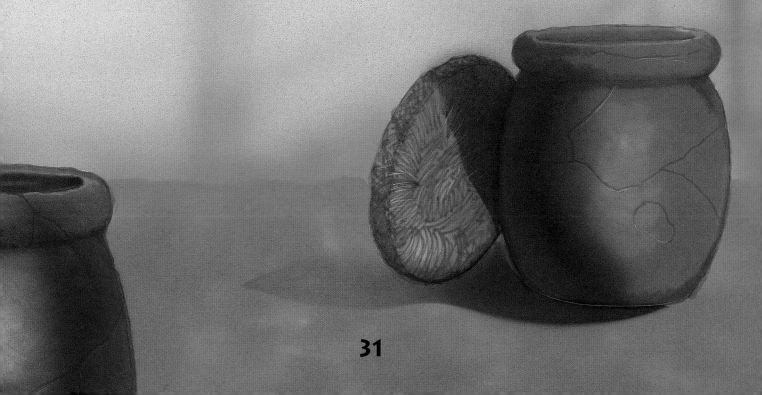

ELEPHANT AND THE RAIN GOD

One day, Elephant said to the rain god, "I know you make trees and plants grow. But what if I tear them all up?"

"If I stop sending rain, nothing will grow," the rain god replied. "What will you do then?"

Elephant decided to challenge the rain god and tore up all the trees and plants. So the god sent no rain for days and weeks, until Elephant was dying of thirst. Then he was forced to beg and plead for water. At last the rain god sent a few showers, just enough to fill a water hole.

After Elephant had quenched his thirst, he ordered Tortoise to guard the water hole for him, so that others could not drink. But soon

Lion came along and scared Tortoise away, before drinking his fill. Then the other animals joined in and soon there was no more water.

So what did Elephant learn? Never challenge nature, and always share with others.

HONEY-BIRD AND THE BROTHERS

Two brothers were out hunting when they came across an upside-down clay pot. The older boy was afraid and left the pot, but his brave brother turned it over. Inside was a little old woman, who jumped out and banged the ground with a stick. With each blow a goat appeared, until there was a small herd. Then the magic woman vanished.

The brothers led the goats toward their village, stopping only for water. The cowardly boy helped his brother down a cliff to a river, but then an evil thought came to him. He dropped the rope and left his brother stranded. When he got home with the goats, he told his father that his brother had run away.

Just then a honey-bird hovered overhead, fluttering and singing. The father followed the bird, who led him to the river and helped him save his brave son. And the cowardly brother? He was forced to leave the village in disgrace.

TORTOISE AND BABOON

One day, Baboon invited Tortoise for dinner. It took Tortoise a long time to get there, and when he did, he knew he had been tricked. Baboon pointed to the top of a tree. "There's our dinner," he giggled, bounding up the tree. "Come and get it!"

Tortoise was no tree-climber, so he had a long, hungry walk home. On his way he decided to get back at Baboon. The next day he invited Baboon for lunch.

There were a lot of bush fires that year, and Tortoise lived beside a large patch of burned and blackened earth. When Baboon arrived for lunch, Tortoise told him off. "Your paws are as black as soot. Run to the river and wash them."

Baboon did as he was told, but then he had to cross the burned patch and get his paws dirty again. Tortoise sent him away, and so it went on until Baboon finally gave up. Tortoise enjoyed his lunch.

FINGER-SIZED FEREYEL

A wicked witch had ten beautiful daughters. In a nearby village lived a woman with eleven sons, who were keen to meet the girls. Their mother warned them that many young men had disappeared when visiting the sisters. But the boys soon set off for the witch's house.

They decided to leave Fereyel, the eleventh son, behind. Fereyel, who was only the size of his mother's thumb, pestered them until they let him go too.

The brothers and sisters got along well, and that night the witch held a party. She gave the boys a strong potion to drink, which made them drowsy. Little Fereyel, who did not drink it, stayed awake and was horrified to see the witch sharpening a big knife outside the window.

Fereyel quickly awakened his brothers and warned them. Just as the witch came bursting in, they all ran out of the back door. When the boys reached home safely, they thanked Fereyel, their thumb-sized hero.

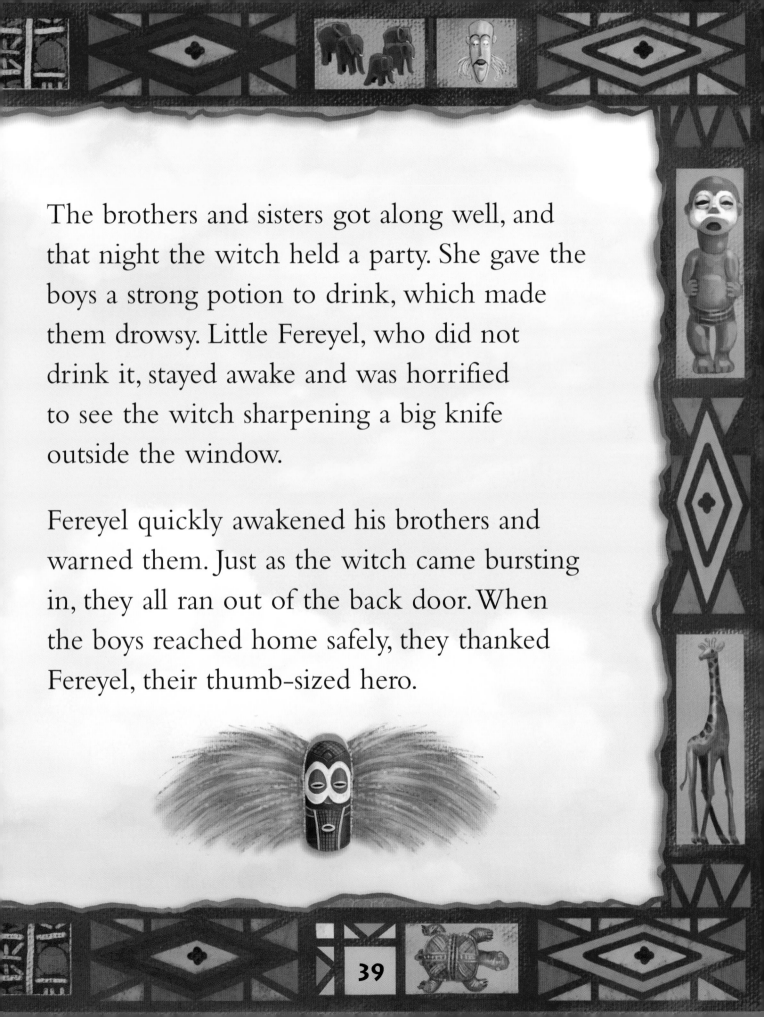

CLEVER, LAZY RABBIT

Rabbit hated hard work, and he was prepared to work hard to avoid it. When his corn needed planting, Rabbit went to Elephant and said, "We should all help each other, don't you think? If you push down the trees, I'll burn them." Elephant agreed.

Later, Rabbit went to Giraffe and said, "I've pushed down the trees. If you burn them, I'll dig the ground." Giraffe agreed.

Next, Rabbit went back to Elephant and said, "I've burned the trees. If you dig the ground, I'll sow the seeds."

Then Rabbit went to Giraffe … and you can guess the rest.

When it came to harvest time, Rabbit went to find Elephant. "If you cut the corn," he said, "I'll gather it in."

Then he found Giraffe and said, "I've cut the corn. Could you gather it in?"

When all the work was done, Rabbit sat down comfortably and wondered why elephants were so big, giraffes so tall and rabbits so very clever.

WHY MONKEYS LIVE IN TREES

Bush Cat was so tired after a day's hunting that she fell asleep at the foot of a tree. When mischievous Monkey saw the cat, he crept up and tied her tail to the tree.

When she woke up, Bush Cat struggled for ages to unravel her tail and get free. She guessed that it was Monkey who had played the trick on her, and she decided to teach him a lesson. So she called all her animal friends together and told them what to do.

"On the fifth day from now," she said, "tell everyone that I am dead and that you are going to bury me."

Five days later, the animals did as their friend asked. Bush Cat lay on the ground, pretending to be dead. All the animals stood around sadly, including Monkey. Suddenly Bush Cat jumped up and sprang at Monkey, who raced up a tree in terror. And that's where monkeys have lived ever since.

WHO'S WHO IN AFRICAN MYTHS

ANANSI

The famous spider character comes originally from myths of the Ashanti people of present-day Ghana. Anansi is a trickster and a hero, sometimes human or half-human – a Spider Man.

BUSH CAT

This is another name for the serval of southern Africa. This wild cat has long legs, large ears and a black-spotted tawny coat.

FEREYEL

The eleventh brother is in the tradition of tiny people that runs through many mythologies. Fereyel is a character of the Fulani people of West Africa.

HONEY-BIRD

This small African bird feeds on honey and beeswax. People followed it to find bees' nests. It was seen as a magical, helpful bird.

KINTU

According to the Baganda people of Uganda, Kintu was the first person on earth and so the father of all people. He was created by the Baganda sky god, Ggulu.

LION

Lion is always seen as the King of Beasts. He is brave, strong and commanding. But all animals can be tricked, and Lion was fooled by clever little Hare.

OBATALA

In the myths of the Yoruba people of Nigeria and Benin, Obatala is the god who created the world and made human bodies. His father Olorun then breathed life into them.

OLOKUN

Olokun features in the myths of several West African peoples. As the goddess of the ocean, she represents several different qualities, including patience, anger and deep wisdom.

OLORUN

In Yoruba mythology, Olorun is the sky god and creator of the universe. He is a god of peace and harmony and is the father of Obatala. He is sometimes seen as female.

ORUNMILA

The great Yoruba god of knowledge and wisdom, Orunmila was created by Olorun, like all the other gods. He helps carry wisdom to earth and its people.

GLOSSARY

bush spirit A ghost or demon that lives in the bush (open countryside).

chameleon A kind of lizard that can change color to suit its surroundings.

continent One of the world's large land masses.

corn A cereal crop, also called maize.

descendant A person related to someone who lived in the past.

forge To shape metal by heating and hammering it.

gourd A large hard fruit used as a bowl.

guinea fowl A plump short-tailed bird.

hornet A stinging insect like a large wasp.

hunter-gatherers People who live by hunting and gathering only, with no crops or livestock being raised for food.

locusts A type of grasshopper found in warm parts of the world. Locusts often move in large swarms that devour crops and vegetation.

myth A traditional story about gods, goddesses, spirits and heroes that often explains how things came about.

ogre An evil monster who eats people.

palm nut The hard-shelled seed of a palm tree.

prehistoric In the time before people made written records.

python A large snake.

sap The sticky fluid that circulates through plants and trees.

savannah Flat grassland with scattered trees.

trickster Someone who likes playing tricks on others.

warthog An African wild pig with tusks.

FURTHER INFORMATION

BOOKS

Arnott, Kathleen. *Tales from Africa*. Oxford University Press, 2000.
Bingham, Jane. *African Art and Culture*. Raintree, 2005.
Parrinder, Geoffrey. *African Mythology*. Chancellor Press, 1996.

WEB SITES

To ensure the currency and safety of recommended Internet links, Windmill maintains and updates an online list of sites related to the subject of this book. To access this list of Web sites, please go to www.windmillbks.com/weblinks and select this book's title.

INDEX

For more great fiction and nonfiction, go to windmillbks.com.